STUDY GUIDE

Regina Swopes
Northeastern Illinois University

APPROACHING DEMOCRACY

THIRD EDITION

Larry Berman
University of California at Davis

Bruce Allen Murphy
Lafayette College

Prentice Hall, Upper Saddle River, New Jersey 07458

© 2001 by PRENTICE-HALL, INC.
PEARSON EDUCATION
Upper Saddle River, New Jersey 07458

ISBN 0-13-088836-2

Printed in the United States of America

Table of Contents

Preface

This Study Guide was designed to accompany the third edition of **Approach Democracy** by Larry Berman and Bruce Murphy. Each chapter contains several self-study sections–defining key terms, multiple choice questions, true/false questions, sentence completions, and finally a number of short answer essay questions. These self-study questions will allow you to test your knowledge of the material from a variety of perspectives. Answers to the questions are given in the final chapter of this guide.

It will of course require additional time and effort on your part to go through this volume answering the questions, and reviewing the material. This manual will be of tremendous benefit to you in obtaining a greater understanding of the material in the text.

Chapter One

Approaching Democracy

Briefly define each of the following terms.

1. affirmative action

2. democracy

3. referenda

4. authoritarian regime

5. direct democracy

6. indirect democracy

7. town meeting

8. interest groups

9. right to privacy

10. stability

11. minority rights

12. pluralism

13. universal suffrage

14. elections

15. political parties

16. free press

17. order

18. judicial review

19. equality

20. representative democracy

21. republic

22. freedom

23. equality of opportunity

24. equality of result

Multiple Choice

25. Democracy could best be defined as a(n)

    a.   authoritarian system.
    b.   monarchy.
    c.   economic system.
    d.   a process of open government.

26. Which of the following were not allowed to vote at the time of the framing of the Constitution?

    a.   women.
    b.   Native Americans.
    c.   African Americans.
    d.   All of the above.

27. The book *Common Sense* was authored by

    a.   Alexander Hamilton.
    b.   Norman Mailer.
    c.   Thomas Paine.
    d.   Thomas Jefferson.

28. All of the following are examples of democracy denied in America except

    a.   the forced segregation and lack of voting rights of African Americans.
    b.   the forced internment of Japanese Americans during World War II.
    c.   the forced relocation of Native Americans.
    d.   the refusal to allow illegal aliens to enter the country.

29. The dissident student movement in 1989 that called itself "pro-democracy' and was crushed by its government occurred in

    a.   China.
    b.   Iran.
    c.   the former Soviet Union.
    d.   North Korea.

30. What feature of democracy was successfully used in the state of Colorado, when it passed an amendment banning state laws protecting gays and lesbians, only to have it overturned in federal court as a result of lawsuits by an opposing coalition?

    a. equality.
    b. majority rule.
    c. organized opposition.
    d. self-government.

31. All of the following would be examples of "freedom to" except

    a. the right to vote.
    b. the right to legal counsel.
    c. the right to equal protection under the law.
    d. the right to speak out against a political official.

32. The type of equality that would redistribute goods and services from the haves to the have-nots is called

    a. equality of relativity.
    b. equality of opportunity.
    c. equality of results.
    d. equality of establishment.

33. In a democratic system, a group becomes the majority by

    a. forcing people to adhere to the wishes of the group.
    b. persuading others to their side by popular input and rational argument.
    c. passing laws to prevent alternative rival groups from forming.
    d. All of the above.

34. Who is the final arbiter of the Constitution?

    a. The president.
    b. The Congress.
    c. The Supreme Court.
    d. The Media.

True or False

35. T   F   In a democracy, voters designate a small number of people to represent their interests; those representatives then meet in a legislative body and make decisions on behalf of the entire citizenry.

36. T   F   Indirect democracy works well for small, homogenous groups of people.

37. T   F   An authoritarian regime is one in which government is apart from the people, oppressing the public by depriving them of basic civil and political liberties.

38. T   F   The framers chose representative rather than direct democracy because of the fear that pure democracy would mean rule by the mob.

39. T   F   To ensure negative freedom, government is expect to do nothing.

40. T   F   Even though Americas has become more democratic than the framers envisioned, the basic structure of government they established still endures.

41. T   F   The reason the United States is said to be approaching democracy is that it has tried but fallen short of upholding core democratic values, such as freedom and equality.

42. T   F   The American military is controlled by the civilian government.

43. T   F   The unique power for the Supreme Court established in the case of Marbury v. Madison was original jurisdiction.

44. T   F   President Harry Truman was able to fire General Douglas MacArthur for insubordination during the Korean War due to the American tradition of a commitment to preserve freedom and equality.

Fill-in-the-Blanks

45. _____ _____ assumes that people can govern themselves.

46. Seeking to keep their new democratic system from committing suicide, the framers decided to create a _____.

47. Democracy in Athens emphasized face-to-face _____ _____ and decision making.

48. _____ _____ implies freedom from government intervention.

49. Every society, to be successful, must maintain _____ and provide social _____.

50. Continual competition among groups in a democracy ensures that power moves around in a _____ _____ of interests.

51. The institution of _____ _____ is the requirement that everyone must have the right to vote.

52. The institutions that most clearly allow people to influence government are _____.

53. The idea that government must stay out of the personal lives of citizens stems from the belief that we all have an inherent _____ _____.

54. A _____ government, using the state to maintain total control over all citizens, suppresses open communication so as to maintain an iron grip over the minds of its populace.

Short Answer Essay

55. Define democracy.

56. Compare and contrast direct democracy with indirect democracy.

57. Describe a republican government.

58. Describe Athenian democracy.

59. List and discuss the core values of democracy.

60. Explain how freedom and equality can be contradictory.

61. Describe the different kinds of equality.

62. Explain how a concern for order and stability can conflict with freedom and equality.

63. Explain why and how democracies seek to balance majority rule with minority rights.

64. Describe the historical expansion of the democratic values of participation in America.

65. List and describe the institutional elements of democracy.

Chapter Two

The Founding And The Constitution

Briefly define each of the following terms

1.   republic

2.   bicameral legislature

3.   sovereignty

4.   social contract theorists

5.   limited government

6.   confederation

7.   Sugar Act

8.   Stamp Act

9.   Townshend Revenue Acts

10.   Boston Tea Party

11.   Committees of Correspondence

12.   Boston Massacre

13.   Intolerable Acts

14.   First Continental Congress

15.   Second Continental Congress

16.   *Common Sense*

17.   Declaration of Independence

18.   Articles of Confederation

19.   Virginia Plan

20.   legislative branch

21. executive branch

22. judiciary

23. separation of powers

24. checks and balances

25. proportional representation

26. council of revision

27. New Jersey Plan

28. unicameral legislature

29. supremacy clause

30. Connecticut compromise

31. three-fifths compromise

32. electoral college system

33. federalism

34. delegated powers

35. reserved powers

36. police powers

37. devolution

38. necessary and proper clause

39. Federalists

40. Antifederalists

41. factions

42. Bill of Rights

43. proposal

44. ratify

45. judicial review

46. supermajority

Multiple choice

47. The proprietary colonies

    a. were ones in which self-government was not allowed to exist.
    b. were thinly disguised religious dictatorships.
    c. were based on royal grants to an English nobleman who determined the nature of the colonial government.
    d. quickly proved to be impractical and were transformed into independent entities.

48. The most influential social contract theorist was

    a. Thomas Hobbes.
    b. John Locke.
    c. William Home.
    d. David Ricardo

49. The document that explained the colonists' reasons for renouncing allegiance to Britain was the

    a. Declaration of Causes and Necessity of Taking Up Arms.
    b. Declaration of Independence.
    c. Proclamation of Rebellion.
    d. Declaration of the Rights of Man.

50. Among the major problems of the Articles of Confederation were all of the following, except

    a. the national government could collect taxes.
    b. the national government had no money to pay for an army.
    c. the executive branch was too powerful.
    d. the government could not enforce its laws.

51. Reserved powers are those given

    a. to state governments.
    b. exclusively to the federal government.
    c. to both the states and federal governments.
    d. only to local government.

52. What does Article V of the Constitution explain?

    a. The powers of the executive branch.
    b. The procedure for ratifying the Constitution.
    c. The procedure for amending the Constitution.
    d. The guidelines for interstate relations.

53. According to James Madison, the source of factions was

    a. the difference in philosophical attitudes between elites and the masses.
    b. the unequal divisions and types of property.
    c. political parties and their respective leaders.
    d. the repression of the minority by the ruling majority.

54. All of the following constitutional amendments had the purpose of expanding rights and equality, except the

    a. Thirteenth Amendment.
    b. Fourteenth Amendment.
    c. Eighteenth Amendment.
    d. Nineteenth Amendment.

55. The most recently added amendment to the Constitution deals with

    a.   granting the right to vote to 18 year olds.
    b.   the prohibition of poll taxes.
    c.   the granting of electoral votes to Washington D.C. residents.
    d.   the delay of congressional pay raises until the following session.

56. Which of the following nations has been most faithful in observing the principles contained in the U. S. Constitution?

    a.   India.
    b.   China.
    c.   Japan.
    d.   Hungary.

True or False

57.   T   F   The Mayflower Compact, signed on November 21, 1620 provided the basis for civil government.

58.   T   F   The United States has a unicameral legislature.

59.   T   F   The notion of equality under the law was John Locke's most significant contribution to social contract theory.

60.   T   F   The Intolerable Acts were passed by the British Parliament in response to Shays' Rebellion.

61.   T   F   The Intolerable Acts forced the colonists to submit to the will of King George III.

62.   T   F   A successful outcome for the Constitutional Convention would have been impossible without a compromise on the slavery issue.

63.   T   F   Vertical powers refer to the system of separation of powers among the three branches of the federal government.

64.   T   F   Police powers are regulated by the states.

65. T   F   The Antifederalists argued that the states should remain independent and distinct, rather than be led by a supreme national government.

66. T   F   The addition of a Bill of Rights to the Constitution was necessary for the document's ratification.

Fill-in-the-Blanks

67. A system of government that allows indirect representation of the popular will is a _____.

68. The independence and self-government of a political entity is a _____.

69. A _____ _____ is a type of government in which the powers of the government are clearly defined and bounded, so that governmental authority cannot intrude in the lives of private citizens.

70. The _____ _____ _____ were a series of acts imposed by the British Parliament in 1767 on glass, lead, tea, and paper imported into the colonies.

71. The _____ _____ _____ were later replaced by the current constitution due to problems inherent in strong centralization.

72. The goal of the _____ _____ _____ was to protect the interests of the smaller, less populous states.

73. Using the _____ _____ _____ to select a person for the office of chief executive, each state gets one elector for each of its representatives and Senators.

74. The relationship between the centralized national government and the individual state governments is called _____.

75. The first ten amendments to the Constitution added in 1791 are known as the _____ _____ _____.

76. The Antifederalist party would later evolve into the _____ party.

Short Answer Essay

77. Briefly describe how early Americans thought about democracy.

78. Describe the actions of the First Continental Congress.

79. Explain the importance of Thomas Paine's *Common Sense*.

80. Explain the actions of the Second Continental Congress.

81. List the major political ideas of the Declaration of Independence.

82. Explain the causes of the American Revolution.

83. Describe the powers of Congress under the Articles of Confederation.

84. Describe the problems under the Articles of Confederation.

85. Describe the issues at the Constitutional Convention that divided the delegated and how they were finally resolved.

86. Describe the provisions in the 1789 Constitution that related to slavery.

87. List the various checks that the branches of the national government can exercise on each other.

88. Give the names and examples of the powers of the national and state governments.

89. List the seven Articles of the Constitution and give a brief description of each.

90. Explain how the 1787 Constitution was unlike any seen before.

91. Describe the characteristics of the delegates to the Constitutional Convention.

92. List the names and views of those delegates who played a major role in drafting the United States Constitution.

93. Describe the differences between the Virginia Plan and the New Jersey Plan.

94. Explain the differences between the Federalists and Antifederalists.

95. Explain how the Constitution has managed to remain vibrant and current even though it has been amended only 27 times.

Chapter Three

Federalism

Briefly define each of the following terms

1. federalism

2. triad of powers

3. supremacy clause

4. delegated powers

5. implied powers

6. inherent powers

7. reserved powers

8. police powers

9. concurrent powers

10. McCulloch v. Maryland

11. Gibbons v. Ogden

12. nullification

13. dual federalism

14. cooperative federalism

15. incorporation

16. grants-in-aid

17. conditions of aid

18. categorical grant

19. formula grant

20. project grant

21. formula/project grant

22. block grants

23. devolution revolution

24. federal mandates

25. creative federalism

26. New Federalism

27. general revenue sharing

28. special revenue sharing

Multiple Choice

29. All of the following would be examples of federalism in action, except

    a. a state providing money for a state park system.
    b. national funding for state and local police forces.
    c. local floods leading to calls for national emergency assistance.
    d. state and national funds being provided to build a road in a state.

30. The form of government in which all power is vested in a central government authority is called

    a. federalism.
    b. a unitary system.
    c. a confederation.
    d. None of the above.

31. The Social Security Act was implemented to provide economic security for those over the age of 65 and unemployment insurance. This demonstrates what advantage of federalism?

    a. Policy diversity.
    b. Dispersal of power.
    c. Minimal policy conflict.
    d. Prospects for governmental experimentation.

32. The ability of the federal government to regulate the racial discrimination practices of restaurants is based on the

    a. First Amendment.
    b. Tenth Amendment.
    c. interstate commerce clause.
    d. habeas corpus clause.

33. What did Congress use as the basis for the Civil Rights Act of 1964?

    a. Interstate commerce power.
    b. The Tenth Amendment.
    c. The supremacy clause.
    d. The general welfare clause.

34. The primary way the general welfare clause has been used to expand national powers is through the national government

    a. directing operating anti-poverty programs.
    b. forcing state governments to operate the anti-poverty programs.
    c. regulating civil rights policies of state governments.
    d. giving money to states to operate programs according to national standards.

35. What powers are delegated specifically to the national government by the Constitution?

    a. Inherent powers.
    b. Reserved powers.
    c. Delegated powers.
    d. Implied powers.

36. The implied powers

    a. have been declared unconstitutional by the Supreme Court.
    b. are constricted to the states by the Fourth Amendment.
    c. can be inferred from delegated powers and justified by the elastic clause.
    d. are based on the power to ratify amendments to the Constitution.

37. The first major issue that caused conflict between national and state governments was the

    a. power to declare war against Britain.
    b. creation of a national bank.
    c. forced eviction of the eastern American Indians to west of the Mississippi River.
    d. purchase of the Louisiana Territory.

38. The view of federalism that holds each level as being supreme within its own jurisdiction is called

    a. dual federalism.
    b. creative federalism
    c. exploratory federalism.
    d. rudimentary federalism.

True or False

39. T F   The framers of the Constitution wanted to create a federal system that had clear, distinct, inflexible allocations of powers between the central and sate governments.

40. T F   One of the advantages of federalism is that it can allow a great deal of diversity among policies and programs to accommodate the diverse population.

41. T F   One disadvantage of federalism is policy diversity, which tends to increase policy conflict.

42. T F   The general welfare clause has been used to protect state powers.

43. T F   After the Civil War, the prevailing view of federalism was one of dual federalism.

44. T F   Categorical grants are the most common grants-in-aid.

45. T F   Although the intention of Nixon's general revenue sharing system was intended to return power to the states, the GRS in fact further extended the influence of the national government.

46. T F   The major goals of Carter's federalism proposals were to target funds to the areas with the greatest need and to encourage more private investment in social problems.

47. T F The Supreme Court and lower court rulings have recently begun to redefine federalism in the direction of more state power.

48. T F Conservative Republicans advocate a state-centered approach, arguing that solutions are best left either to state governments or to the private sector.

Fill-in-the-Blanks

49. The rights that have neither been granted to the national government nor forbidden to the states by the Constitution are called _____ _____.

50. The _____ _____ _____ is made up of three constitutional provisions that help to continually shift the balance of power between the national and state governments.

51. Congress used the _____ _____ _____ approach to achieve near uniformity on the new legal drinking age of twenty-one.

52. The _____ clause in the Article VI of the Constitution holds that in any conflict between federal laws and treaties and state laws, the will of the national government always prevails.

53. _____ _____ are those powers not assigned by the Constitution to the national government but left with the states or the people, according to the Tenth Amendment.

54. _____ _____ regulate health, morals, public safety, and welfare, which are reserved to the states.

55. A nineteenth-century theory which holds that states faced with unacceptable national legislation can declare such laws null and void and refuse to observe them is called _____.

56. The process whereby the protections of the Bill of Rights have been found by the Supreme Court to apply to the states is called _____.

57. A _____ _____ is a national requirement that must be observed.

58. The _____ is the most frequently used federal grant.

Short Answer Essay

59. Define the various ways in which a central government of a nation is related to the smaller governing units.

60. Explain the advantages of federalism.

61. Discuss the disadvantages of federalism.

62. Discuss how the interstate commerce clause has affected federalism.

63. Explain how the general welfare clause has affected federalism.

64. Discuss the impact of the Tenth Amendment upon federalism.

65. List the various types of powers the Constitution assigns to each level of government and give examples of each.

66. List those powers which the Constitution denies to both the national and state governments.

67. Explain the constitutional disagreements between Hamilton and Jefferson concerning the national governments authority to create a bank.

68. Discuss the importance of McCulloch v. Maryland.

69. Compare and contrast dual federalism with cooperative federalism.

70. Describe important judicial decisions concerning federalism after the New Deal Era.

71. List and describe the various kinds of federal grants.

72. Describe the characteristics of creative federalism.

73. Compare and contrast "new federalism" with "*new* new federalism."

74. Describe federalism under the Bush administration.

75. Describe federalism under the Clinton administration.

Chapter Four

Congress

Briefly define each of the following terms

1. bicameral legislature

2. necessary and proper clause

3. reapportionment

4. redistricting

5. gerrymandering

6. majority-minority district

7. delegates

8. trustees

9. incumbents

10. franking privilege

11. casework

12. term limits

13. "two congresses"

14. Speaker of the House

15. House majority leader

16. party caucus

17. minority leader

18. whip

19. President of the Senate

20. president pro tempore

21. Senate majority leader

22. standing committees

23. select or special committees

24. conference committees

Multiple Choice

25. The Constitution gives Congress authority in the following areas, except

   a.   local governmental affairs, such as crating cities and counties.
   b.   economic affairs, such as coining money.
   c.   domestic affairs, such as regulating interstate commerce.
   d.   foreign affairs, such as declaring war.

26. In regard to representativeness,

    a.   Congress is much more ethnically diverse than just a few decades ago.

    b.   the membership of Congress accurately reflects America's different social groups.

    c.   the Senate is much more representative of the variety of America's social groups than the House.

    d.   wealthy representatives are unable to represent adequately the interests of the poor.

27. The size of the House of Representatives is

    a.   established at 100 by the Constitution.

    b.   established after each census and fluctuates between 400 and 500.

    c.   set by legislation at 435.

    d.   set by tradition bo be four times the size of the Senate.

28. Representatives who would follow their constituents when voters have clear preferences and their own best judgement when the electorate is unsure are called

    a.   brokers.

    b.   politicos.

    c.   dynamos.

    d.   despots.

29. Incumbents have the following advantages, except

    a.   financial.

    b.   franking privilege.

    c.   lack of voting record to defend.

    d.   legislative experience.

30. Who is the president of the Senate?

    a.   The president of the United States.

    b.   The Senate majority leader.

    c.   The Speaker of the House.

    d.   The vice president of the United States.

31. What type of committee is formed to reconcile differences between the versions of a bill passed by the House and the Senate?

    a. Standing committee.
    b. Select committee.
    c. Joint committee.
    d. Conference committee.

32. What is the most commonly used procedure in the House Rules Committee?

    a. Open rules.
    b. Closed rules.
    c. Restrictive rules.
    d. Waiver of rules.

33. A major difference between the House and Senate procedural rules is that

    a. in the House, all amendments must be germane to the bill.
    b. in the Senate, all amendments must be germane to the bill.
    c. the House allows interest group representatives to speak on a bill before the floor.
    d. the Senate allows the president to give testimony to the Senate floor on the crucial bills.

34. Cloture requires approval of

    a. two-thirds of those present
    b. two-thirds of the entire Senate.
    c. three-fifths of the entire Senate.
    d. a simple majority of those present.

True or False

35. T   F   House membership is more stable than that of the Senate.

36. T   F   Congress has increased the ethnic diversity of its membership as a result of Supreme Court decisions and the redistricting that has taken place at the state level.

37. T   F   The Supreme Court has ruled that although race can be a factor in redistricting, it cannot be the overriding consideration.

38. T   F   Representatives from marginal districts that could go either way electorally tend to vote according to personal opinion rather than constituency views.

39. T   F   The advantage of incumbency is a relatively recent phenomenon.

40. T   F   Congress as an institution has generally been held in high regard by the public.

41. T   F   The position of president pro tempore is essentially honorary, carrying little political clout.

42. T   F   Since both houses of congress jealously guard their independence and prerogatives, congress established only a few joint committees.

43. T   F   The House is smaller, more decentralized, and more informal than the Senate.

44. T   F   Only members of Congress can introduce a bill.

Fill-in-the-Blanks

45.   The _____ _____ _____ clause of the Constitution, also called the elastic clause, has been interpreted by the Supreme Court to allow Congress to develop its role broadly with regard to regulating commerce, borrowing money, and collecting taxes.

46.   A process or redrawing voting district lines from time to time and adjusting the number of representatives allotted each state is called _____.

47.   Any attempt during sate redistricting of congressional voting boundaries to create a safe seat for one party is called _____.

48. Congress members who feel authorized to use their best judgement in considering legislation see themselves a _____.

49. Individuals who currently hold public office are _____.

50. A legislated limit on the amount of time a political figure can serve in office is knows as _____ _____.

51. The American public's view of Congress has generally had a "Love my congressman, hate the Congress" view of the institution, know as the _____ _____ phenomenon.

52. Much of the legislative work of Congress is done is _____, the smaller work groups that consider and draft legislation.

53. A traditional form of the logrolling norm is called _____ _____, special interest spend for members' districts or states.

54. When a member of Congress drafts and submits a piece of legislation dealing with a particular issue, that issue is said to be on the _____ _____.

Short Answer Essay

55. Explain why Congress is considered the world's most powerful legislature.

56. Describe the differences between the House of Representatives and the Senate.

57. List the broad areas of powers of Congress and give examples of each.

58. List the factors that limit Congress's power.

59. Describe the characteristics of those typically serving in Congress.

60. Explain how reapportionment, redistricting, and gerrymandering are related.

61. Compare and contrast the roles of delegate and trustee.

62. List the reelection rates of incumbents and explain the advantages which explain them.

63. Describe the public's view of Congress and individual congresspersons.

64.   Describe how a bill becomes a law.

65.   Describe the key leadership positions in the House and the Senate.

66.   List the different types of committees in congress and give an example of each.

67.   Explain why Congress uses committees.

68.   Give three reasons why congresspersons seek membership on a particular committee.

69.   Describe the changes adopted in the 1970's that affected committees.

70.   Describe how measures are brought to the floor on the House and Senate.

71. Describe how filibusters work, can be ended, and their affect on democracy.

72. Discuss the informal rules and norms of Congress.

73. List and explain those factors which determine why members of Congress vote as they do.

74. List six ways a member of Congress could stop the passage of a bill.

Chapter Five

The Presidency

Briefly define each of the following terms

1. veto

2. pocket veto

3. treaties

4. executive agreement

5. executive privilege

6. stewardship

7. constructionist

8. line item veto

9. going public

10. chief of staff

11. Executive Office of the President

12. cabinet

13. vice president

Multiple Choice

14. The president has a fixed term of office, serving

    a. two years.
    b. four years.
    c. six years.
    d. eight years.

15. What Amendment restricts the president to two terms of office?

    a. Eighteenth.
    b. Nineteenth
    c. Twenty-second.
    d. Twenty-fifth.

16. Which of the follow presidents issued the greatest number of vetoes during his tenure in office?

    a. Franklin D. Roosevelt.
    b. Richard M. Nixon.
    c. John F. Kennedy.
    d. Harry S. Truman.

17. Formal international agreements between sovereign states are called

    a. treaties.
    b. lateral understandings.
    c. executive agreements.
    d. joint resolutions of Congress.

18. What foreign policy tool did Theodore Roosevelt use to restrict Japanese immigration to the United States?

    a. Treaties.
    b. Executive agreements.
    c. Lateral understandings.
    d. Joint resolutions of Congress.

19. What is the most important specific power granted to the president by the Constitution?

    a. Veto power.
    b. Executive privilege.
    c. Appointment power.
    d. Commander-in-Chief of the Armed Forces.

20. What presidential role is illustrated in the president calling out the National Guard to lend assistance during the North Dakota floods of 1996?

    a. Crisis leader.
    b. Chief diplomat.
    c. Chief of state.
    d. Chief legislator.

21. The president visits with leaders from other countries to maintain good relations with allies. This illustrates what presidential role?

    a. Chief of state.
    b. Chief diplomat.
    c. Chief executive.
    d. Commander-in-chief.

22. Which is a true statement about the War Powers Resolution?

    a. The Resolution's effectiveness at limiting presidential action has been proved by the historical record.
    b. The Resolution was passed over President Nixon's veto in 1973.
    c. The president does not have to consult Congress until some sixty days after she has ordered troops into combat overseas.
    d. None of the above.

23. The Brownlow Commission dealt with the issue of

    a. presidential war-making powers.
    b. permanent staffing for the president.
    c. improving communications between the president and the public.
    d. None of the above.

True or False

24. T F   The president has a central role in the legislative process through the power of the veto.

25. T F   The Constitution gives presidents the power to negotiate treaties with other nations.

26. T F   Only 1 percent of all treaties submitted to the Senate have actually been defeated.

27. T F   Executive agreements allow presidents to make important foreign policy moves without Senate knowledge or approval.

28. T F   The Constitution makes no reference to party leadership.

29. T F   In comparison to domestic policy, presidents traditionally have great leeway and independence in their conduct of foreign policy.

30. T F   The constitutionality of the legislative veto was upheld in *INS v. Chadha*.

31. T F   In the past few decades, it has become evident that a congressional declaration of war is no longer needed for a president to send American troops into combat.

32. T F   "Going public" is a strategy that recent presidents have scrupulously avoided.

33. T F   The cabinet does not legally exist.

Fill-In-The-Blanks

34.   Under the Constitution, the selection of the president is made by the _____ _____.

35.   Formal international agreements between sovereign states are called _____.

36.   Diplomatic contracts negotiated with other countries that allow presidents to make important foreign policy moves without Senate approval are called _____ _____.

37.   The relationship between international crisis and presidential support has become know as the _____ _____

38.   A classic example of the _____ model of presidential power is illustrated in President Roosevelt's ordering the U.S. seizure of Panama and the subsequent building of the Panama Canal.

39.   The view of presidential power espoused by William Howard Taft was the _____ view.

40. The _____ _____ _____ allows the president, within one week of passage, to eliminate specific parts of spending or tax bills without having to block the entire bill.

41. The _____ _____ _____ of 1973 requires that the president report to Congress within 48 houses after committing U. S. troops to hostile action.

42. The _____ _____ _____ is responsible for the operation of the White House, plays a key role in policy-making, and acts as gatekeeper to the president.

43. The _____ _____ is the second highest elected official in the United States.

Short Answer Essay

44. Describe the great paradox of the American presidency.

45. Describe the seven key principles upon which the framers based the presidency and the reasons behind them.

46. List the constitutional requirements for becoming president.

47. List and describe the formal powers given to the president in the Constitution.

48. List and describe the informal, or functional roles of the president.

49. Discuss the concept of executive privilege and its use over time.

50. Explain why the office of Independent Counsel was created and discuss how it has functioned in recent years.

51. Explain the difference between the stewardship approach to executive power and the constructionist approach.

52. Explain why trends favor occupants of the White House being activist individuals.

53. Explain the "three sub-presidencies" which comprise the president's job description.

54.   Explain the real issue behind the line item veto.

55.   Describe those factors that have resulted in the enlargement of presidential powers.

56.   Describe presidential war powers.

57.   Trace the development of a president's "going public" to further their goals.

58.   Trace the development of the institutionalized presidency.

59.   Explain the role and function of the cabinet.

60.   Explain the role and function of the vice president.

61.   Describe the challenges of presidential leadership.

62. Describe how the framers' design of the presidency has been altered.

Chapter Six

The Judiciary

Briefly define each of the following terms

1. original jurisdiction

2. appellate jurisdiction

3. Marbury v. Madison

4. judicial review

5. statutory construction

6. trial court

7. appellate jurisdiction

8. criminal cases

9. plea bargains

10. civil cases

11. class action suit

12. constitutional courts

13. U. S. District courts

14. U. S. Courts of appeals

15. en blanc

16. legislative courts

17. docket

18. writ of certiorari

19. rule of four

20. solicitor general

21. amicus curiae briefs

22. briefs

23. opinion

24. majority opinion

25. plurality opinion

26. concurring opinion

27. dissenting opinion

28. stare decisis

29. precedents

30. judicial restraint

31. judicial activism

32. senatorial courtesy

Multiple Choice

33. The Supreme Court is the most undemocratic of the three branches because

    a.   it operates in total secrecy.
    b.   its justices are appointed rather than elected.
    c.   the justices have almost total power to say what the law is.
    d.   All of the above.

34. What Article of the Constitution outlines the nature of the federal judicial branch?

    a.   Article I.
    b.   Article II.
    c.   Article III.
    d.   Article IV.

35. The power of the Court to interpret federal or state law and apply it to particular case is called

    a.   literary exposition.
    b.   judicial imperialism.
    c.   legal jurisprudence.
    d.   statutory construction.

36. What power is used most frequently by the Supreme Court?

    a. Judicial review.
    b. Interpreting the meaning of a statue and applying it to a specific case.
    c. Issuing writs of mandamus.
    d. Refusing to review cases.

37. All of the following points about appellate courts are true except

    a. usually appellate courts have multi-judge panels and no jury.
    b. appellate courts will consider only points of law.
    c. appellate courts will have additional witnesses and evidence to decide the guilt or innocence of the defendant.
    d. the ruling of appellate courts could lead to a new trial if they decide that the lower court had ruled incorrectly on points of law.

38. The U.S. court of appeals consists of how many courts?

    a. 3.
    b. 4.
    c. 13.
    d. 50.

39. What type of court is the U.S. Tax Court?

    a. Trial court.
    b. Appellate court.
    c. Legislative court.
    d. District court.

40. What percent of the appointees to the Supreme Court have been from the president's own political party?

    a. 50 percent.
    b. 70 percent.
    c. 80 percent.
    d. 90 percent.

41. Which of the following presidents have dramatically changed the direction of the Court?

    a. Kennedy.
    b. Nixon.
    c. Reagan.
    d. All of the above.

42. The recent law school graduates who serve as assistants to Supreme Court Justices are called

    a. judicial fellows.
    b. law apprentices.
    c. legal eagles.
    d. law clerks.

True or False

43. T F   There is a strong correlation between judicial independence and democratic government.

44. T F   The appellate court considers only matters of law.

45. T F   Legislative court judges are appointed for life.

46. T F   Presidents tend to be bipartisan in their judicial appointments.

47. T F   If a Supreme Court appointment comes early in a president's term or during a period of presidential popularity, the Senate is more likely to allow a nomination to succeed.

48. T F   The Supreme Court never explains why it accepts or rejects cases.

49. T F   The judicial conference takes place in total secrecy, with only the justices present.

50. T F   A concurring opinion is one that a justice writes when she agrees strongly with the majority opnion and wants to reinforce the impact of their decision on society.

51. T F   Federal and state courts are supposed to follow Supreme Court precedents in making their own decisions.

52. T F   In actuality, Congress does not have any effective way to show discontent when the Supreme Court interprets a congressional action to ways Congress disapproves.

Fill-in-the-Blanks

53.   When a court hears cases already argued and decided by another court, it has _____ jurisdiction.

54.   The usual point of original entry into the legal system, with a single judge and jury deciding both fact and law, is called _____ court.

55.   A _____ _____ suit refers to large groups of people joining together in a civil case in which the results are applicable to all participants.

56.   A procedure in which a president submits the names of judicial nominees to senators from the same political party who are also from the nominee's home sate for their approval prior to formal nomination is called _____ _____.

57.   The Supreme Court's agenda is called a _____.

58.   In what is known as the _____ _____ _____, a vote by at least four justices to heat the case will grant the petition for a writ of certiorari and put the case on the Court's docket.

59.   A written version of the decision of a court is the _____.

60.   When a justice disagrees with the holding of the court, frequently he or she will write a _____ _____, speaking for that justice alone or a few of the members of the Court.

61.   A doctrine meaning "let the decision stand" is called _____ _____.

62. Judges who practice _____ _____ believe that they have a duty to reach out and decide issues even to the point, some critics charge, of writing their own personal values into law.

Short Answer Essay

63. Discuss the issues raised in the *Bowers v. Hardwick* case.

64. Explain why the judicial branch of the national government was originally considered the least dangerous and why this view has changed.

65. Describe the powers of the U.S. Supreme Court.

66. List the constitutional provisions that were designed to keep the Supreme Court independent.

67. List ways in which the judiciary is influenced by outside forces.

68. List the two types of federal and state courts and the two types of cases they hear.

69. Describe the organization of the federal courts.

70. Describe the process for appointing federal judges and the political factors that affect the appointment process.

71. Give the reasons why the U.S. Senate might refuse to confirm a nominee to the Supreme Court.

72. Explain why the Senate has sought greater influence in the confirmation process and give the steps the president has taken to counteract this.

73. Describe the impact of Presidents Kennedy, Nixon, Reagan, and Clinton on the Supreme Court.

74. Describe how recent presidents have sought to leave their mark on the composition of the federal courts.

75. Give the factors the Court considers when selecting which cases to decide.

76. Give the reasons for the Court's shrinking docket.

77. Describe the process of the Court for deciding cases.

78. List and describe the factors which explain the Court's ruling.

79. Explain how the Supreme Court's decisions are implemented.

80. Explain the role of public opinion implement Supreme Court decisions.

Chapter Seven

The Bureaucracy

Briefly define each of the following terms

1. bureaucracy

2. bureaucrats

3. specialization

4. hierarchy

5. formal rules

6. welfare state

7. spoils system

8. civil service

9. hatch Act

10. implementation

11. administrative discretion

12. administration

13. regulation

14. cabinet departments

15. independent agencies

16. independent regulatory commissions

17. government corporation

18. appointment power

19. Office of Management and Budget

20. iron triangles

21. issue networks

22. red tape

23. privatization

Multiple Choice

24. Americans usually measure bureaucratic performance by

    a.   cost of service.
    b.   speed of delivery of service.
    c.   quality of the service compared to the private sector.
    d.   impact of bureaucratic failure.

25. People are concerned and suspicious about bureaucracy mainly because

    a.   it costs so much.
    b.   bureaucrats are so unrepresentative of the public.
    c.   it is hard to control bureaucracy and hold it accountable for its action.
    d.   there are so many obvious examples of failures to perform adequately.

26. What president is linked to the spoils system?

    a. Andrew Jackson.
    b. James Monroe.
    c. Theodore Roosevelt.
    d. Harry Truman.

27. The bureaucracy performs all of the following governmental tasks, except

    a. regulation.
    b. centralization.
    c. administration.
    d. implementation.

28. A good example of federal bureaucratic regulation would be

    a. delivering the mail.
    b. collecting entry fees from each international airline passenger.
    c. building and flying the space shuttle.
    d. enforcing the anti-discriminatory guidelines of the Equal Employment Opportunity commission.

29. All of the following are examples of independent regulatory commissions, except the

    a. Federal Communications Commission.
    b. Federal Reserve Board.
    c. Export-Import Bank.
    d. Federal Trade Commission.

30. Among the constraints on bureaucratic behavior are all of the following, except

    a. bureaucratic agencies do not control their own revenue.
    b. the rules as to how to deliver services are established elsewhere.
    c. bureaucratic goals are mandated by other units of government.
    d. the heads of most bureaucratic agencies are publicly elected.

31. The friendly, interdependent relationship between Congress and certain federal agencies is called the

   a. devil's duo.
   b. cozy coterie.
   c. iron triangle.
   d. steel magnolia.

32. The agency that is the nation's chief covert operations and information gathering bureau is the

   a. National Security Agency.
   b. State Department Councillor Service.
   c. Central Intelligence Agency.
   d. Bureau of External Intelligence Resource.

33. What is the excessive amount of rules and regulations that government employees must follow called?

   a. Red tape.
   b. Iron law.
   c. Multiplicity of agents.
   d. Spoils system.

True or False

34. T F   Although New Deal programs were designed as temporary emergency programs to relieve the suffering of the Depression, most agencies became a permanent part of an enlarged federal bureaucracy.

35. T F   The great majority of federal employees work in or near the national capital, Washington, D.C.

36. T F   The routine task performed by bureaucrats to achieve a specific policy goal is called administration.

37. T F   Federal bureaucratic agencies are actually more a part of the legislative branch than of the executive.

38. T F Independent agencies are usually smaller than cabinet departments and have a narrower set of responsibilities.

39. T F Independent agencies regulate a sector of the nation's economy in the public interest.

40. T F The Federal Deposit Insurance Corporation is an independent regulatory commission.

41. T F Congress does not allow agencies to keep money left over when the fiscal year ends.

42. T F Privatization involves securing the confidentiality of government records on individual private citizens.

43. T F Bureaucratic organizations are inherently undemocratic.

Fill-in-the-Blank

44. A clear chain of communication and command running from an executive director at the top down through all levels of workers is called a

_____.

45. In a bureaucracy, _____ _____ govern the execution of all tasks within the jurisdiction of a given agency.

46. The _____ _____ is a social system whereby the government assumes primary responsibility for the welfare of citizens.

47. A system in which government jobs and contracts are awarded on the basis of party loyalty rather than social or economic status of relevant experience is called the _____ _____.

48. The system of hiring and promoting employees based on professional merit is called _____ _____.

49. _____ is the actual execution of a policy.

50. Major administrative units whose heads are presidential advisers appointed by the president and confirmed by the Senate are

_____ _____.

51. The informal three-way relationships that develop among key legislative committees, the bureaucracy whose budgets are supervised by those committees, and interest groups with a vested interest in the policies created by those committees and agencies are called _____ _____.

52. The Civil Service Reform Act of 1978 created the _____ _____ _____, a group of upper-management bureaucrats with access to private-sector incentives such as bonuses but also subject to measurable job-performance evaluations.

53. The turning over of public responsibilities to privately owned and operated enterprises for regulation and for providing goods and services is called _____.

Short answer essay

54. Describe bureaucracy and give three ways a bureaucracy promotes efficiency.

55. Describe the problems inherent in the bureaucratic form.

56. Trace the growth of the federal bureaucracy.

57. Describe how the character of the bureaucracy has changed over the years.

58. Explain the purpose of the Hatch Act and how it has been amended in recent years.

59. List and describe the three key government tasks performed by the bureaucracy.

60. List and briefly describe the four government institutions that constitute the federal bureaucracy.

61. List the factors that impede the bureaucracy's ability to do its job.

62. Describe how presidents may control the bureaucracy.

63. Describe how Congress may control the bureaucracy.

64. Describe some problems associated with the FBI and the CIA.

65. Give the public's opinion of the government bureaucracy.

66. Evaluate the criticisms of the federal bureaucracy.

67. Give the various reforms that have been proposed for the federal bureaucracy.

Chapter Eight

Public Policy

Define each of the following terms

1. public opinion

2. straw poll

3. respective sampling

4. margin of error

5. random sample

6. sampling bias

7. tracking polls

8. exit polls

9. political socialization

10. generational effect

11. gender gap

12. political culture

13. political ideology

14. culture theory

15. schemas

16. realignment

17. intensity

18. latency

19. salience

Multiple Choice

20. James Madison would argue that

    a.   public opinion should always be heeded.
    b.   public opinion should always be totally ignored.
    c.   public opinion should be taken into account, but not followed slavishly.
    d.   None of the above.

21. In a random sample

    a.   every member of the population must have an equal chance of appearing in the sample.
    b.   only men should be questioned.
    c.   only women should be questioned.
    d.   only voters should be questioned.

22. Close-knit families produce offspring whose political views

    a.   are very similar.
    b.   are very diverse.
    c.   are extremely conservative.
    d.   are extremely liberal.

23. The issue of school prayer in public schools

    a.   has never been an issue in the United States.
    b.   is only important to Muslims.
    c.   is highly controversial.
    d.   has been resolved.

24. The effect of social class upon political views

    a.   has always been clear.
    b.   has proven very difficult to measure.
    c.   has changed throughout history.
    d.   has only been measured in Canada.

25. In general, minorities

    a. distrust society and public authorities.
    b. often feel alienated from society.
    c. vote less frequently than those in the majority.
    d. All of the above.

26. Jones University is become infamous for

    a. its ban on gay students.
    b. called the Catholic Church a "Satanic Cult."
    c. referring to the Pope as an "anti-christ."
    d. All of the above.

27. Which is America's most conservative region?

    a. The South.
    b. The Northeast.
    c. The Midwest.
    d. Florida.

28. As a well-informed citizenry, Americans

    a. are about average for democracies.
    b. fall short.
    c. are up to par on some issues, and totally ignorant on others.
    d. are very well versed on public issues.

29. Party identification

    a. is still very strong in America.
    b. is a good predictor of an individual's political behavior.
    c. determine how a political candidate is evaluated.
    d. None of the above.

True or False

30. T F   It is generally held that no president can respond to every change in public opinion.

31. T F   Opinion polls are not an important aspect of American politics.

32. T F   The generation of the 1960's differ markedly from the generation of the 1940's.

33. T F   Hispanics tend to vote overwhelmingly Republican.

34. T F   Members of any country's dominant religion tend to be more liberal.

35. T F   People living in rural areas are generally more conservative.

36. T F   The gender gap refers to the difference in political opinions between men and women.

37. T F   One of the core values of American society is political inequality.

38. T F   Many Americans do not identify themselves as either liberal or conservative.

39. T F   Schemas are religious frameworks for evaluating the world.

Fill-in-the-Blanks

40.   The main problem with most polls is that they fail to achieve a
_____ _____.

41.   Attention to _____ _____ is important for reliable results.

42.   _____ _____ are used by the media to trace the support levels of candidates over time.

43. Liberal critics fault the schools for perpetuating social divisions, and for filing to teach about _____ and

_____.

44. More than anything else, _____ has emerged to dominate the social and political landscape.

45. Generally, the more religious one is the more _____ one tends to be.

46. The leading American value is _____.

47. _____ _____ is a coherent way of viewing politics and government.

48. A _____ is an intellectual framework for evaluating the world.

49. _____ is a measure of the depth of feeling associated with a given opinion.

Short Answer Essays

50. Explain the flaws in the Literary Digest's presidential poll in 1936.

51. Define public opinions and give different views concerning it's proper role

52. What are the major factors involved in measuring public opinion?

53.   Explain the importance of polls.

54.   List the major institutions of political socialization and the contribution of each.

55.   What are the major social variables which influence the formation of public opinion?

56.   List and discuss the core values of America's political culture.

57.   Are Americas intolerant? Discuss.

58.   What are the major political ideologies in America.

59.   Discuss how politically aware and involved most Americans are.

60.   Discuss the debate over the nature of American political opinions.

61. What is the relationship between public opinion and public policy?

Chapter Nine

Political Parties

Briefly define each of the following terms

1. political parties

2. realignment

3. Revolution of 1800

4. King Caucus

5. primary system

6. New Deal coalition

7. recruitment

8. local party organization

9. state party organization

10. machine politics

11. national party organization

12. national party convention

13. party platform

14. nomination

15. caucus

16. primary election

17. winner-take-all system

18. proportional representation

19. closed primary

20. open primary

21. frontloading

22. McGovern-Fraser Commission

23. superdelegates

24. political action committees

25. multi-party system

26. single-member districts

27. electoral college

28. party identification

29. minor or third parties

Multiple Choice

30. A nongovernmental institution that organizes and gives direction to mass political desires in the pursuit of power is called a(n)

    a.   interest group.
    b.   mass media organization.
    c.   think tank.
    d.   political party.

31. A significant historical event that causes major shifts in party identification and loyalty is called

    a.   party realignment.
    b.   party reduction.
    c.   party amalgamation.
    d.   bipartisan cooperation.

32. What was the first election in which popular votes were counted and the last to be settled by the House of Representatives?

    a.   1800.
    b.   1804.
    c.   1824.
    d.   1932.

33. What American political party espoused many of the ideals of the French Revolution, such as the idea of direct popular self-government?

    a.   Whigs.
    b.   Democrats.
    c.   Jeffersonians.
    d.   Federalists.

34. What is the most basic role of parties?

    a. To raise money for party employees.
    b. To nominate candidates and win elections.
    c. To offer comfort to people confused by the political process.
    d. To fight for ideologically distinct policy preferences.

35. In trying to find out what voters want and giving it to them, parties are carrying out their

    a. representation function.
    b. inductive function.
    c. demagogic function.
    d. least important function.

36. The major task of the national party organization is to

    a. organize the national party conventions every four years.
    b. select the presidential and vice presidential candidates every four years.
    c. draft the party platform that all party nominees must pledge to support.
    d. All of the above.

37. Meetings of party adherents who gather to discuss and deliberate, and then give their support to a candidate for president are called

    a. caucuses.
    b. open primaries.
    c. closed primaries.
    d. blanket primaries.

38. What type of primary allows cross-party voting?

    a. Open primary.
    b. Closed primary.
    c. Caucus.
    d. Blanket primary.

39. The single-member district electoral system inhibits the development of

    a. third parties.
    b. interest groups.
    c. coalitions
    d. political action committees.

True or False

40. T   F   Political parties are not mentioned in the Constitution.

41. T   F   Today's Democratic party, a direct descendant of Jefferson's party, is the oldest political party in the world.

42. T   F   Where parties are weak, interest groups are strong.

43. T   F   Party activists are wealthier and better educated than the population at large.

44. T   F   The Democrats are more effective at fund-raising than the Republicans.

45. T   F   Americans have tended to prefer primary elections, which are more inclusive and democratic in nature than caucuses.

46. T   F   The open primary is used by most states.

47. T   F   Two states, Washington and Alaska, have blanket primaries.

48. T   F   Cross-party voting is possible in closed primaries.

49. T   F   Interest groups have recently declined in their influence.

Fill-in-the-Blanks

50.   Nongovernmental institutions that organize and give direction to mass political desires are called _____.

51.   The first election in the world in which one party (the Federalist party of John Adams) willingly gave up power because of a lost election to another party (the Republican party of Thomas Jefferson) without bloodshed was called the _____.

52.   The process of selecting candidates for president in the early nineteenth century in which the members of each party's delegation in Congress did the nominating was known as the _____.

53.   The _____ is a system of nominating candidates in which voters in each state make the choice by casting ballots.

54.   An organizational style of local politics in which party bosses traded jobs, money, and favors for votes and campaign support was called _____.

55.   The _____ is the statement of principles and policies, the goals that a party pledges to carry out if voters give it control of the government.

56.   In the _____ system, the winner of the primary or electoral college vote gets all of the state's convention or electoral college delegates.

57.   In the _____ primary, only citizens registered as members of a particular political party may participate in that party's primary.

58.   Delegates to the Democratic National Convention who are not bound to vote for any particular candidate are called _____.

59.   The group of 538 electors who meet separately in each of their states and the District of Columbia on the first Monday following the second Wednesday in the December after a national presidential election to officially elect the president and the vice president of the United States are called the _____.

Short Answer Essay

60.   Describe the functions political parties perform.

61.   Give a brief description of the five party systems.

62. Give the evidence for and against the assertion that there was a 6th realignment after 1968.

63. List and explain why the United States has a two-party system.

64. Explain why minor parties appear.

65. Describe the performance of minor parties.

66. List the functions of minor parties.

67. Describe the various levels of party organization.

68. Give five reasons why the old machine systems of politics declined during the 20th century.

69. Describe the process by which a Democrat or a Republican becomes a candidate for president.

70. Discuss the various attempts to reform the nomination process since 1968.

Chapter Ten

Participation, Voting, And Elections

Briefly define each of following terms

1. participation

2. poll tax

3. literacy test

4. voter turnout

5. initiative

6. referendum

7. party identification

8. split-ticket ballots

9. straight party ticket

10. retrospective voting

11. protest

12. civil disobedience

13. political violence

14. midterm elections

15. coattail effect

16. electoral college

17. faithless elector

18. contingency election

19. maintaining election

20. deviating election

21. realigning election

22. dealignment

23. federal matching funds

24. soft money

25. issue advocacy

26. independent expenditures

Multiple Choice

27. In summarizing the participation levels of the American citizens, one can conclude that

    a. very few Americans are active to any degree in politics.
    b. close to half of the population is engaged in some form of serious, politically oriented activity.
    c. nearly all Americans are active participants in political life.
    d. None of the answers are correct.

28. Many political observers measure the health of a democracy by the degree to which citizens participate in elections. This is referred to as

    a. voter turnout.
    b. voter pullover.
    c. voter mobility.
    d. electoral responsiveness rate.

29. The one overwhelming influence on voting decisions is

    a. region of residence.
    b. sex and sexual preference.
    c. party identification.
    d. religion.

30. The powerful form of issue voting where voters look back over the last term to judge how well the incumbent candidate or party has performed is called

    a. retrospective voting.
    b. two-pronged voting.
    c. rational analysis voting.
    d. rudimentary voting.

31. A major new way of becoming informed about politics and organizing political events is

    a. two-way closed circuit television.
    b. forming highly organized group cells, much like the old communist party did.
    c. electronic mail and the Internet.
    d. personal columns in daily newspapers.

32. The 1998 election was called a

   a. contingency election.
   b. maintaining election.
   c. midterm election.
   d. presidential election.

33. To be officially elected president one must

   a. receive a majority of the total electoral college votes.
   b. have both the highest popular vote total and win a majority of the total electoral college votes.
   c. win a majority in a congressional vote of confidence and investiture.
   d. win a plurality of total electoral college votes.

34. How many electoral votes does a winning candidate need to receive the required majority?

   a. 50
   b. 200
   c. 270
   d. 538

35. The major strategy in a presidential campaign is

   a. raising the most money possible for a television commercial blitz.
   b. not alienating any vital voter group.
   c. going where the votes are, to the big states.
   d. adhering to every Federal Election Commission rule in order to avoid decertification.

36. What are independent expenditures?

   a. Funds spent by independent candidates or minor parties
   b. Funds a candidate spends to cover the costs of fund-raising
   c. Funds now outlawed by a recent Supreme Court ruling
   d. Funds spent by a group for a cause and not coordinated with a candidate.

True or False

37. T F   The U.S. Supreme Court has ruled that the motor-voter law was an infringement on the states right to govern.

38. T F   Political activists are largely well-educated, middle and upper-income white voters.

39. T F   The United States has the highest level of voter turnout among all democratic countries.

40. T F   Younger people are more likely to vote than older people.

41. T F   Initiatives are submitted by a state legislature to the public for popular vote.

42. T F   About 70 percent of the electorate vote a straight-party ticket.

43. T F   The 1992 and 1996 presidential elections provide strong support for the retrospective voting model.

44. T F   To become president, the winning candidate must receive 270 of the 538 electoral votes.

45. T F   Only about 55 percent of the electorate turn out to vote for president.

46. T F   Regional realignment has occurred in the South, particularly among males who formerly supported the Republican party and now are solidly Democrats.

Fill-in-the-Blanks

47.   One technique designed to keep African Americans from voting was the _____, a fee that had to be paid before one could vote.

48.   The percentage of eligible voters who actually show up and vote on election day is referred to as _____.

49.   An _____ is a proposal submitted by the public and voted upon during elections.

50.   Ballots on which people vote for candidates of only one party are called _____ tickets.

51.   A powerful form of issue voting in which voters look back over the last term or two to judge how well an incumbent or the in party has performed in office is called _____.

52.   Elections in which Americans elect members of Congress but not presidents are called _____.

53.   A member of the electoral college who casts his or her vote for someone other than the states popular voter winner is called the _____.

54.   An election in which the majority party of the day wins both Congress and the White House is called a _____ election.

55.   Contributions used by state and local party organizations for party building activities are called _____.

56.   A loophole in the campaign finance law involving no limits to funds that are dispersed independently by a group or person in the name of a cause, presumably not by a candidate, involves _____.

Short Answer Essay

57.   Briefly trace the history of voting in the United States.

58. Describe the different amounts of political participation in the U.S. and characteristics of people at each level.

59. List the steps taken to keep blacks from voting after passage of the Fifteenth Amendment.

60. Describe the levels of voter turnout in congressional and presidential elections.

61. Give the explanations for poor turnout in U.S. elections.

62. Give the institutional explanations for why Americans do not register to vote.

63. Give the psychological explanations for why Americans do not register to vote.

64. Give the variables affecting who votes.

65. Define initiative and referendum and describe how successful they have been.

66. Describe the factors that determine for whom people vote.

67. Identify the factors that must be present for issue voting to occur.

68. Describe ways of participating in politics other than voting.

69. Explain the coattail effect.

70. Give the reasons for the framers designing the electoral college.

71. Explain how the electoral college works today.

72. Give the proposals for reforming the electoral college and the pros and cons of each proposal.

73. Describe how the strategy for winning the presidency changed during the 1960s.

74. Explain the statement, "Americans tend to elect 'plurality' presidents."

75. Describe the provisions of the 1974 Federal Elections Campaign Act.

76. Describe the effects of the 1974 campaign finance reforms.

Chapter Eleven

Interest Groups

Briefly define each of the following terms

1. interest groups

2. actual groups

3. potential groups

4. policy entrepreneur

5. political action committees

6. collective action

7. public interest groups

8. group maintenance

9. free riders

10. lobbying

11. grass-roots activity

12. soft money

13. iron triangle

14. gridlock

15. policy networks

Multiple Choice

16. Americans have long been noted for their propensity to

    a. wage war.
    b. participate in elections.
    c. join groups.
    d. None of the above.

17. Interest groups that have already been formed are called

    a. potential groups.
    b. active groups.
    c. actual groups
    d. policy initiators.

18. Which of the following would not be considered a liberal group?

    a. The American Civil Liberties Union.
    b. The National Organization of Women.
    c. The National Rifle Association.
    d. The National Association for the Advancement of Colored People.

19. The information provided by interest groups tends to be

    a. biased.
    b. totally wrong.
    c. primarily religious in nature.
    d. None of the above.

20. The United States Chamber of Commerce has an annual budget of

    a. 10 million dollars.
    b. 20 million dollars.
    c. 65 million dollars.
    d. 129 million dollars.

21. Religious groups are a type of

    a. civil rights group.
    b. ideological group.
    c. business group.
    d. All of the above.

22. The National Abortion Rights Action League is an example of a(n)

    a. single-issue group.
    b. business group.
    c. a and b.
    d. a only.

23. Members who do not invest but still share in the collective benefits of group action are know as

    a. free riders.
    b. loafers.
    c. leaders.
    d. None of the above.

24. The first political action committee was created in

    a. 1980.
    b. 1974.
    c. 1972.
    d. 1948.

25. Interest group activity is protected by the

    a. Second Amendment.
    b. Tenth Amendment.
    c. Nineteenth Amendment.
    d. First Amendment.

True or False

26. T F   Potential groups are groups that have already been formed.

27. T F   Madison believed that interest group activity was a logical consequence of human nature.

28. T F   There were no interest groups in the United States prior to the 1980's.

29. T F   Interest groups are primarily concerned with the poor and disadvantaged.

30. T F   The most common type of groups are business groups.

31. T F   The book *Unsafe At Any Speed* was authored by Jimmy Carter.

32. T F   Interest groups want to be government, not merely influence government.

33. T F   Interest group leaders spend a great deal of time engaged in group maintenance.

34. T F   Today there are fewer than 1500 lobbyists.

35. T F   Interest group lobbying is limited to Congress.

Fill-in-the-Blanks

36.   Madison believed that the power of actions could be moderated by _____ their influence.

37.   People form and join groups because _____ _____ is stronger, more credible, and more likely to influence policy outcomes than the isolated actions of individuals.

38.   One of the most interesting developments in American government since the 1960's is the dramatic increase in _____
_____ _____.

39.   _____ _____ interest groups are organizations that represent citizens who are primarily concerned with one particular policy or social problem.

40.   Group leaders must devote a major portion of their time to _____
_____.

41.   For lobbyists, _____ is crucial.

42.   Groups use _____ _____ to target citizens with mailings describing the group's cause.

43.   _____ is the formal, organized attempt to influence legislation.

44.   Campaign contribution directed to advancing the interests of a political party or an issue in general, rather than a specific candidate is called _____ _____.

45.   Political scientist _____ _____ argued that interest groups played a stabilizing role in American politics.

Short Answer Essays

46. What is an actual group?

47. What is a potential group?

48. What was James Madison's view of interest groups?

49. Describe the growth of interest groups since the 1970's.

50. What are the functions of interest groups?

51. List and discuss the different types of interest groups.

52. Describe the factors that influence the development of interest groups.

53. Discuss the free-rider problem.

54. Give the various differences in interest groups that help explain their different levels of success.

55. What are the various strategies used by interest groups?

56. Explain the growth of political action committees, and the problems associated with them.

57. Discuss the various attempts to regulate interest groups.

58. What role to interest groups play in American politics?

Chapter Twelve

The Media

Briefly define each of the following terms

1. spin

2. mass media

3. muckraking

4. yellow journalism

5. investigative journalism

6. socialization

7. Federal Communications Commission

8. equal time rule

9. fairness doctrine

10. right of rebuttal

11. prior restraint

12. libel

13. sound bite

Multiple Choice

14. The job of the media is to

    a. transmit information
    b. simplify complex details into symbols and images.
    c. Both of the above.
    d. Neither of the above.

15. The term "yellow journalism" is derived from

    a. a type a paper used to publish newspapers.
    b. a comic strip character.
    c. news stories which occur in the late evenings.
    d. newspapers with a yellow mark on the front.

16. Roughly how many Americans now own televisions?

    a. 34 percent.
    b. 56 percent.
    c. 80 percent.
    d. 98 percent.

17. Social scientists generally agree that the mass media perform which of the following functions?

    a. Surveillance of world events.
    b. Interpretation of events.
    c. Socialization of individuals into cultural settings.
    d. All of the above.

18. Investigative journalism is different from yellow journalism in

    a. the amount of time spent on a particular story.
    b. investigative journalists are paid more money.
    c. newspapers which feature yellow journalism are sold only in grocery stores.
    d. Investigative journalism makes greater use of technology.

19. The Federal Communications Commission was created in

    a. 1912 after the sinking of the Titanic.
    b. 1934.
    c. 1965.
    d. 1990.

20. Which of the following is not a guideline which the electronic media must follow?

    a. A rule limiting the number of stations an individual or organization may own.
    b. A rule mandating public-service programing.
    c. A rule that older journalists must be paid more than younger journalists.
    d. A rule promising to protect the rights of individuals.

21. During presidential campaigns the media tends to focus on

    a.   the issues.
    b.   the election rules.
    c.   the candidates.
    d.   the voters.

22. Which of the following would not be done by a candidate attempting to counter negative advertising?

    a.   Defending against the charges.
    b.   Attacking the credibility of the accuser.
    c.   Ignoring the attack.
    d.   Quitting the race.

23. The most successful use of radio by a politician was

    a.   Nixon's "Checkers Speech."
    b.   Roosevelt's "Fireside Chats."
    c.   Clinton's "Weekly Address."
    d.   Lincoln's "Gettysburg Address."

True or False

24. T   F   Democracy requires that most governmental activities be kept secret.

25. T   F   The term spin derives from sports.

26. T   F   Newspapers were not widely read until the 1980's.

27. T   F   Television coverage of new events tends to be very slow.

28. T   F   The term narrowcasting was coined by Ed Murrow.

29. T   F   The media never interprets the news, they only report.

30. T   F   There is a correlation between exposure to mass media and a person's fear of violent crime.

31. T F The media is protected by the Fifteenth Amendment.

32. T F Opinion polls are rarely used these days.

33. T F There is no evidence that the media significantly affects public opinion.

Fill-in-the-Blank

34. The Federalist Papers were published in the New York
_____ _____.

35. The most widely read news magazine is _____.

36. The sprit of the muckraker can still be seen in the practice of
_____ _____.

37. The media plays an important role in the process by which people learn to conform to the society's norms and values. This is called
_____.

38. Americans take pride in the tradition of a _____
_____.

39. The _____ _____, now abandoned, required radio and television stations to provide a reasonable percentage of time for programs dealing with issues of public interest.

40. Governmental suppression of information is known as _____
_____.

41. The relationship between the media and the government is often termed as _____.

42. The media has been accused of focusing on the _____
_____ nature of politics.

43. Over the years _____ have become progressively shorter.

Short Answer Essays

44.   Discuss the controversy over the proper relationship between the media and democracy.

45.   Trace the evolution of the mass media in America.

46.   What has been the consequence of new technology on the media?

47.   What has been the impact of talk radio?

48.   Describe the three basic functions of the mass media.

49.   Discuss the limits placed upon the mass media.

50.   Describe how the Federal Communications Commission regulates the media.

51. What is prior restraint?

52. Is the media biased? Discuss.

53. How can a candidate counter negative advertising?

54. Discuss the media's role in the election process.

55. Discuss political advertising.

Chapter Thirteen

Civil Liberties

Briefly define each of the following terms

1. civil liberties

2. civil rights

3. incorporation

4. no incorporation

5. total incorporation

6. clear and present danger test

7. double jeopardy

8. selective incorporation

9. Lemon test

10. secular regulation rule

11. least restrictive means test

12. fighting words

13. hate speech

14. symbolic speech

15. prior restraint

16. subsequent punishment

17. slander

18. libel

19. exclusionary rule

20. probable cause

21. Miranda warning

Multiple Choice

22. Civil liberties are guaranteed by

    a. state laws.
    b. some state constitutions.
    c. the Bill of Rights and the due process clause of the Fourteenth Amendment.
    d. the Seventh Amendment.

23. Cases involving civil liberties nearly always come down to conflict between the

    a. church and state.
    b. individual and state.
    c. corporation and individuals.
    d. local government and federal governments.

24. An approach in which the states would be bound only by the dictates of due process contained in the Fourteenth Amendment was called

    a. incorporation.
    b. no incorporation.
    c. total incorporation.
    d. selective incorporation plus.

25. The clear and present danger doctrine of Justice Holmes

    a.   states that the circumstances and nature of speech could justify its restriction.
    b.   was applied to cases involving speech that might hinder the war effort.
    c.   was later abandoned by Holmes.
    d.   All of the above.

26. Double jeopardy is banned by the

    a.   First Amendment.
    b.   Fourth Amendment.
    c.   Fifth Amendment.
    d.   Sixth Amendment.

27. Some actions, such as burning the American flag, take the place of speech and are commonly called

    a.   substitute speech.
    b.   hate speech.
    c.   symbolic speech.
    d.   fighting words.

28. What amendment provides for the right to be represented by counsel?

    a.   Fourth Amendment
    b.   Fifth Amendment
    c.   Sixth Amendment
    d.   Eighth Amendment

29. In *Katz v. United States*, the scope of the Fourth Amendment was extended to include

    a.   police searches.
    b.   grand jury testimony.
    c.   electronic eavesdropping.
    d.   double jeopardy.

30. The Fifth Amendment includes all of the following, except the

    a.   right not to be compelled to be a witness against yourself in a criminal trial.
    b.   protection against double jeopardy.
    c.   protections against cruel and unusual punishment.
    d.   right to a speedy and public trial by an impartial jury.

31. According to the text, the right to obtain an abortion

    a.   is likely to be overturned soon by the Court.
    b.   appears to be secure with the current composition of the Court.
    c.   is not considered a binding precedent by the current Court.
    d.   will disappear with the next Supreme Court appointment.

True or False

32. T   F   The Supreme Court has ruled that flag-burning is protected as symbolic speech.

33. T   F   Civil rights are derived largely from the Bill of Rights and the due process clause of the Fourteenth Amendment.

34. T   F   Cases involving civil liberties almost always derive from a conflict between the individual and the state.

35. T   F   The Supreme Court has ruled that slander and libel are protected by the First Amendment.

36. T   F   Gag orders barring the media from publishing information about an ongoing criminal case are very common today.

37. T   F   As it stands now, the Supreme Court will not allow attempts to regulate alleged pornography on the Internet.

38. T   F   Loopholes in the exclusionary rule, such as the good faith exception, seriously weaken the guarantee of privacy implied in the Fourth Amendment.

39. T   F   Prisoners on death row are disproportionately black, and almost all are male.

40. T F   The right of privacy is not explicitly mentioned in the Constitution.

41. T F   For now, the right to obtain an abortion, though restricted in some cases, seems secure.

Fill-in-the-Blanks

42.   The approach in which the Bill of Rights would be absorbed into the due process clause by the simple act of redefinition was called the _____ of the Bill of Rights.

43.   A free speech test allowing states to regulate only speech that has an immediate   connection to an action states are permitted to regulate is called the _____.

44.   Being tried twice for the same crime is called _____; it is banned by the Fifth Amendment.

45.   The _____ test emerged from the Supreme Court case Lemon v. Kurtzman in 1971.

46.   The _____ rule holds that there is no constitutional right to exemption, on free exercise grounds, from laws dealing with nonreligious matters.

47.   Certain expressions are so volatile that they are deemed to incite injury. They are not protected under the First Amendment and are thus referred to as _____.

48.   Speech or symbolic actions intended to inflict emotional distress, defame, or intimidate people is called _____.

49.   _____, such as burning the American flag, takes the place of speech because they communicate a message.

50.   _____ is an action in which the government seeks to ban the publication of controversial material by the press before it is published.

51. The _____ warning must be recited by police officers to a suspect before questioning.

Short Answer Essay

52. Compare and contrast civil liberties with civil rights.

53. Explain how the civil liberties protections in the Bill of Rights were applied to states.

54. Explain the "clear and present danger" test.

55. Describe early Supreme Court decisions (1925-1934) dealing with incorporation.

56. Describe incorporation after 1937.

57. Describe how the Supreme Court has decided "establishment of religion" cases.

58.   Describe how the Supreme Court has decided "free exercise of religion" cases.

59.   Describe the Court's rulings in the area of free speech.

60.   Describe the Court's rulings in the area of freedom of the press.

61.   Describe the Court's rulings in the area of "searches and seizures."

62.   List the rights guaranteed by the Fifth and Sixth Amendments and describe important cases dealing with these rights.

63.   Explain the Court's view on the right to privacy.

64.   Describe the issues raised by and the Court's ruling in the issue of abortion.

Chapter Fourteen

Civil Rights And Political Equality

Briefly define each of the following terms

1. discrimination

2. civil rights

3. de jure equality

4. de facto equality

5. black codes

6. suffrage

7. state action

8. Jim Crow laws

118

9. poll tax

10. peonage

11. desegregation

12. integration

13. civil disobedience

14. boycott

15. protest march

16. sit-ins

17. freedom riders

18. affirmative action

19. equality of opportunity

20. equality of result

21. quota programs

22. sexism

23. test of reasonableness

24. strict scrutiny test

25. heightened scrutiny test

26. equality

Multiple Choice

27. All of the following were federal actions before the Civil War to protect slavery in some way, except the

    a. Wilmot Proviso.
    b. Fugitive Slave Act.
    c. Missouri Compromise.
    d. Compromise of 1850.

28. In the Dred Scott case, the Supreme Court ruled that

    a.   all laws protecting slavery were unconstitutional.
    b.   slavery was permissible in the South but northern states could prohibit slavery if   they chose.
    c.   African Americans had no constitutional rights, and Congress could not prohibit slavery.
    d.   None of the above.

29. All of the following were used by southern states to disenfranchise black voters, except

    a.   property qualifications.
    b.   poll taxes.
    c.   literacy tests.
    d.   occupational tests.

30. The constitutional basis for the case outlawing segregated public schools was the

    a.   First Amendment freedom of speech clause.
    b.   equal protection clause of the Fourteenth Amendment.
    c.   right to vote provision of the Fifteenth Amendment.
    d.   necessary and proper clause of Article I, Section 8.

31. All of the following are examples of civil disobedience, except

    a.   boycott of businesses.
    b.   a protest march down the main street of a city.
    c.   a sit-in at lunch counters.
    d.   bomb threats of public facilities.

32. In the Bakke case, the Supreme Court ruled that

    a.   set quotas in university admissions based solely on race were unconstitutional.
    b.   set quotas of any kind were unconstitutional.
    c.   quotas were acceptable if the applicants from majority groups did not protest.
    d.   quotas were required in some circumstances.

33. According to the text, a major new development in the spread of white supremacist hate groups is the

   a. First Amendment protection of such groups.
   b. controversy of federal law enforcement efforts at Waco and Ruby Ridge.
   c. ease of communicating over the Internet.
   d. increase in TV talk shows.

34. The test of reasonableness

   a. was the traditional standard used by courts in sexual discrimination cases.
   b. was based on whether a reasonable person would agree that a law had a rational basis.
   c. made it very difficult to prove sexual discrimination.
   d. All of the above.

35. Who led the attack on the test of reasonableness?

   a. Sandra Day O'Connor
   b. Thurgood Marshall
   c. Ruth Bader Ginsburg
   d. Alan Dershowitz

36. The text states that American society will have to deal with questions of discrimination and equality with two other groups, which are

   a. Arabs and Asians.
   b. Muslims and Hindus.
   c. white males and the religious right.
   d. the elderly and homosexuals.

True or False

37. T F   Civil liberties are the constitutionally guaranteed rights of the individual that may not be removed arbitrarily by government.

38. T F   The 1857 Dred Scott case had far-reaching implications for the civil rights of women.

39. T   F   The case known as Brown II ordered lower federal courts to enforce desegregation plans in public schools with all deliberate speed.

40. T   F   The Civil Rights Act of 1964 greatly increased the federal governments ability to fight discrimination.

41. T   F   A major complicating factor in trying to end racial discrimination in the North was segregation in the North was de facto, based on non-governmental factors and thus hard   to change by law.

42. T   F   Following the 1969 case of *Alexander v. Holmes County Board of Education*, in which the Court ruled that every school district must desegregate immediately, the South became the most integrated schools in the nation but there was little progress in the northern cities.

43. T   F   Removing legal obstacles does not automatically result in actual equality.

44. T   F   Those in favor of affirmative action argue that because of the effects of past discrimination, true equality could not be achieved until those effects are overcome by transition programs giving minorities temporary advantages.

45. T   F   The Clinton Administration's policy toward civil rights has been ambiguous, sometimes supporting past programs strongly and at other times calling for more study and review.

46. T   F   The strict scrutiny test will make it much easier to uphold federal affirmative action programs.

Fill-in-the-Blanks

47. The constitutionally guaranteed rights that may not be arbitrarily removed by the government, such as the right to vote, are called _____.

48. Equality of results, or _____, measures whether real world obstacles to equal treatment exist.

49. Equality before the law is called _____.

50. _____ laws were passed by Southern states that separated the races in public places.

51. A system in which employers advance wages and then require workers to remain on their jobs, in effect enslaving them, until the debt is satisfied is called _____.

52. The elimination of laws and practices mandating separation of the races is called _____.

53. When a person breaks the law in a nonviolent way and is willing to go to jail in order to publicly demonstrate that the law is unjust, that person is engaging in _____.

54. When protestors refuse to patronize any organization that practices policies that are perceived to be unfair for political, economic, or ideological reasons, they are _____.

55. _____ programs attempt to improve the chances of minority applicants for jobs, housing, employment, or graduate admissions by giving them a boost relative to white applicants with roughly the same qualifications.

56. The idea that people should have equal rights and opportunities to develop their talents that all people should begin at the same starting point in a race defines _____.

Short Answer Essay

57. Define civil rights and explain its importance to democracy.

58.   Describe important legal events pertaining to equality for African Americans from the Constitution to the Civil War.

59.   Describe the Dred Scott case and give its importance.

60.   Explain those actions taken by the government called reconstruction.

61.   Describe the Supreme Court actions pertaining to the rights of African Americans after the Civil War.

62.   Give the actions of presidents during and after World War II concerning desegregation.

63.   Describe the important court rulings dealing with race and education prior to the Brown decision.

64.   Give the Courts reasoning in the Brown decision and state and federal responses to it.

65. Describe the significant events of the civil rights movement.

66. Describe the major provisions of the Civil Rights Act of 1964 and the Voting Rights Act of 1965.

67. Compare and contrast de jure discrimination with de facto discrimination.

68. Describe the issues raised by affirmative action and the history of its use (including Supreme Court decisions).

69. Trace the history of women's rights in America prior to the first Supreme Court case striking down sex discrimination.

70. Describe the Supreme Court cases dealing with laws treating men and women differently.

71. Describe the kinds of discrimination experienced by Hispanic Americans.

72. Describe the kinds of discrimination experienced by Native Americans.

73. Give the forms of discrimination Americans with disabilities face and describe the actions of Congress in this area.

Chapter Fifteen

Public Policy

Briefly define each of the following terms.

1. public policy

2. regulatory policy

3. social welfare policy

4. policy elites

5. public agenda

6. formal agenda

7. issue state

8. triggering mechanism

9.   implementation

10.   policy evaluation

11.   environmental impact statement

12.   entitlement

13.   means testing

14.   workfare

15.   poverty level

16.   policy entrepreneurs

Multiple Choice

17.   Which of the following is not an example of public policy?

    a.   Regulating industry.
    b.   Achieving societal goals.
    c.   National defense.
    d.   Unifying religious organizations.

18. In 1986, the Surgeon General of the United States was

    a.   Margaret Heckler.
    b.   Al Gore.
    c.   C. Everett Koop.
    d.   Ralph Nader.

19. Who has the primary responsibility for the formulation and implementation of public policy?

    a.   Congress
    b.   The Courts.
    c.   Federal agencies
    d.   All of the above

20. The National Environmental Policy Act was passed in

    a.   1969.
    b.   1980.
    c.   1985.
    d.   1998.

21. The largest single non-defense item in the national budget is

    a.   public education.
    b.   social security.
    c.   medical research.
    d.   congressional salaries.

22. The War On Poverty was launched by

    a.   President Jackson.
    b.   President Roosevelt.
    c.   President Johnson.
    d.   President Bush.

23. The poverty level is determined by the

    a.   Census Bureau.
    b.   Department of Agriculture.
    c.   Justice Department.
    d.   Department of Education.

24. According to the text, policy elites would include

    a. members of Congress.
    b. social and civic leaders.
    c. journalists.
    d. All of the above.

25. Regulatory policies have

    a. increased in recent years.
    b. decreased in recent years.
    c. remained the same in recent years.
    d. been declared unconstitutional.

26. Pollution credits were created by

    a. the Kyoto Protocol.
    b. the Civil Rights Act of 1964.
    c. the Clear Air Act of 1990.
    d. the Water Conservation Act of 1995.

True or False

27. T   F   Regulatory policy involves the use of police powers by the federal government.

28. T   F   In 1983 the Centers for Disease Control spent 30 million dollars on AIDS research.

29. T   F   The term logrolling refers to policies that benefit a particular state or district.

30. T   F   The Superfund Law was enacted in 1954.

31. T   F   The national government may regulate the price charged for a good or service.

32. T   F   The EPA was created in 1970.

33. T   F   Social security is an example of an entitlement.

34.   T   F   The money to fund social security comes from a tax placed on cigarettes.

35.   T   F   Social security recipients are subjected to means testing.

36.   T   F   The Medicare Act was passed in 1965.

Fill-in-the-Blanks

37.   In contrast to _____, social welfare policy used positive incentives.

38.   Policy scholars have developed several processes that try to capture the flavor and substance of policy making. Once such model views the policy-making process as a _____.

39.   The _____ is the set of topics that are a source of concern for policy elites, the general public, or both.

40.   American political history offers many examples of _____ _____ who succeeded in placing a potential policy issue on the public agenda.

41.   Following evaluation, policies are either terminated or continued. If they are continued, they enter what social scientists call the _____ _____.

42.   Congress requires that government agencies issue an _____ _____ _____ listing the effects that proposed agency regulations would have on the environment.

43.   The first international conference on the environment was held in 1992 in _____.

44.   The Great Depression acted as a _____ _____ to translate the economic condition of poverty into a political issue to be addressed by policy makers.

45. The other major thrust of the War on Poverty was the _____
_____.

46. The Family Support Act attempted to address the trend toward the
_____ ____ _____.

Short Answer Essay

47. What are the four objectives of public policy?

48. Define the different types of public policy.

49. Describe the policy life-cycle.

50. Explain how an issue becomes part of public agenda.

51. How does an issue become included in the formal agenda?

52. What is the Kyoto Protocol?

53. Why are some policies easier to implement than others?

54. What are the characteristics of an effective public policy?

55. List and discuss the five aspects of policy making that make it a highly political process.

56. Briefly discuss the politics of AIDS.

57. What are the different kinds of regulatory activity in which the national government engages?

58. What are the three sets of concerns relating to future environmental regulation?

59. List and discuss the major programs created during President Johnson's War on Poverty.

60. Describe the major changes that have taken place in welfare programs during the Reagan, Bush, and Clinton administrations.

Chapter Sixteen

Economic Policy

Briefly define each of the following terms

1. economic policy

2. deficit

3. laissez-faire economics

4. Keynesian economics

5. fiscal policy

6. monetarism

7. monetary policy

8. Federal Reserve System

9. supply-side economics

10. stagflation

11. Office of Management and Budget

12. impoundment

13. Congressional Budget Office

14. tariffs

15. progressive taxes

16. regressive taxes

17. capital gains tax

18. tax expenditures

19. excise taxes

20. budget resolution

21. discretionary spending

22. mandatory spending

23. national debt

24. World Trade Organization

25. North American Free Trade Agreement

26. Federal Reserve Board

Multiple Choice

27. What type of government policy has the clearest impact on the economy?

    a. fiscal policy
    b. regulatory policy
    c. monetary policy
    d. international economic policy

28. The economic theory that advocates minimal government involvement, allowing individuals to do as they please, is known as

   a. laissez-faire economics.
   b. mercantilist economics.
   c. Keynesian economics.
   d. minimalist economics.

29. The challenge to the economic policy of minimal government involvement that called for an active government role in the economy is called

   a. laissez-faire economics.
   b. mercantilist economics.
   c. Keynesian economics.
   d. dynamic economics.

30. The founder of the economic theory who urged an activist government to stimulate and manage the economy was

   a. Warren Rudman.
   b. Adam Smith.
   c. John Maynard Keynes.
   d. Vilfredo Pareto.

31. The major function of the Federal Reserve System is to

   a. act as the central bank and overseer of monetary policy.
   b. control the size of the federal government's deficit and debt.
   c. push government and corporation investments into areas of greatest social need and economic promise.
   d. stabilize the interest rate.

32. In general, the Federal Reserve System

   a. is tightly controlled by the president and his economic advisers.
   b. has its budget set by the president and Congress but has some freedom in its choice of policies.
   c. is free of the usual checks and balances and has its own source of revenue.
   d. is controlled and financed by the majority party in Congress.

33. Ronald Reagan took office during a period of

    a. inflation.
    b. deflation.
    c. stagnation.
    d. stagflation.

34. The income tax is an example of a

    a. flat tax.
    b. value-added tax.
    c. progressive tax.
    d. regressive tax.

35. Tax deductions that reduce the amount of income that is subject to taxes, such as home mortgages, are called

    a. tax revenues.
    b. tax liabilities.
    c. tax shelters.
    d. tax expenditures.

36. The key to budget resolution is two broad types of

    a. taxing.
    b. spending.
    c. budgeting.
    d. borrowing.

True or False

37. T   F   Monetarists call for a stable monetary policy, which is controlled by Congress.

38. T   F   Supply-siders emphasize the importance of the business sector.

39. T   F   Budgetary politics involves many actors, the most important being the president and Congress.

40. T   F   Regressive taxes are considered the fairest because they place a larger burden on those people with the greatest ability to pay.

41. T F   Capital gains tax comes mostly from lower-income taxpayers.

42. T F   In general, the greater the number of tax brackets, the more progressive the tax.

43. T F   The Clinton tax reform placed its emphasis on those with the greatest ability to pay.

44. T F   Democrats were blamed for the government shutdown that occurred in 1996 when the deadline passed for budget negotiations.

45. T F   Mandatory spending accounts for 33 percent of all spending and is authorized by permanent laws.

46. T F   When fully implemented in the next several years, NAFTA will make trade among the United States, Canada, and Mexico as free and easy as among the states across America.

Fill-in-the-Blanks

47.   The annual shortfall between the monies that government takes in and spends is the _____.

48.   The primary mechanism for stimulating spending is _____, government efforts to stabilize the economy through the power to tax and spend.

49.   Created in 1913, the _____ is the nation's principal overseer of monetary policy.

50.   Simultaneous high unemployment and high inflation is referred to as _____.

51.   The president's refusal to spend funds appropriated by Congress is referred to as _____.

52.   The _____ is a government office that analyzes budgetary figures and makes recommendations to Congress and the president.

53. The imposition of import taxes on foreign goods in an attempt to protect a nation's industry are called _____.

54. The tax on unearned income from rents, stocks, and interest is called _____.

55. A statement passed by Congress that is the framework for spending decisions is called a _____.

56. _____ spending accounts for 33 percent of all federal spending and is the spending Congress actually controls.

Short Answer Essay

57. List the three primary goals of economic policy and explain the relationship among them.

58. Describe the various theories of domestic economic policy that have been popular throughout U.S. history.

59. Define monetarism and describe the form it takes in the United States.

60. Explain supply-side economics and describe its success under President Reagan.

61. Describe the political process of creating the federal budget.

62. Identify the sources of federal tax dollars.

63. Explain the difference between progressive taxes and regressive taxes.

64. Describe the major provisions of the Tax Reform Act of 1986.

65. Describe Clinton's tax reform proposals.

66. Give the typical breakdown of the government's spending.

67. Explain and give examples of uncontrollable expenditures.

68. Explain the difference between deficit and national debt.

69. Describe the objectives of GATT and the NAFTA Treaty.

70. Explain the need for international policy coordination.

Chapter Seventeen

Foreign Policy

Briefly define each of the following terms

1. foreign policy

2. isolationism

3. Monroe Doctrine

4. superpower

5. containment

6. globalism

7. North Atlantic Treaty Organization

8. Cold War

9. bipolarity

10. Warsaw Pact

11. foreign aid

12. Peace Corps

13. Gulf of Tonkin Resolution

14. detente

15. Strategic Arms Limitation Treaty

16. economic sanctions

17. legislative oversight

18. War Powers Resolution

19. military-industrial complex

Multiple Choice

20. All of the following are core goals of American foreign relations, except

    a. military security.
    b. isolationism.
    c. survival and independence.
    d. economic security.

21. During the post-World War II period, the term superpower applied

    a. only to the United States.
    b. both to the United Sates and the Soviet Union.
    c. to the western and communist alliance systems.
    d. to any nation that developed an atomic bomb.

22. The intention to assist free, democratic nations beat back the threat of totalitarianism became known as the

    a. Monroe Doctrine.
    b. Truman Doctrine.
    c. New World Order.
    d. War Powers Resolution.

23. The U.S. monopoly of nuclear weapons ended in

    a. 1914.
    b. 1945.
    c. 1949.
    d. 1990.

24. The Alliance For Progress program focused on

    a. Africa.
    b. Latin America.
    c. Eastern Europe.
    d. China.

25. The Gulf of Tonkin Resolution granted

    a.   President Nixon authority to initiate a policy of detente.
    b.   President Johnson authority to pursue the war in Vietnam.
    c.   President Kennedy authority to invade Cuba.
    d.   None of the above.

26. President Clinton's Partnership for Peace initiative was concerned with

    a.   negotiating an end to nuclear proliferation under the auspices of the
         United States.
    b.   strengthening NAFTA and expanding it to include other nations in Latin
         America.
    c.   preventing Iraq from again invading Kuwait.
    d.   increased military cooperation and integration as a first step toward
         NATO membership.

27. The Clinton administration has tried to respond to the new global economic
    environment by stressing the policy of

    a.   regionalism.
    b.   globalism.
    c.   enlargement.
    d.   containment.

28. The oldest and most preeminent department of the foreign policy bureaucracy
    is considered to be the Department of

    a.   State.
    b.   Defense.
    c.   Commerce.
    d.   Justice.

29. The first president to openly claim the existence of a military-industrial
    complex was

    a.   Bush.
    b.   Nixon.
    c.   Truman.
    d.   Eisenhower.

True or False

30. T   F   The Monroe Doctrine reinforced isolationism by promising not to interfere in the internal concerns of European states.

31. T   F   The nuclear age began with the U.S. bombing of Hiroshima and Nagasaki in August 1945.

32. T   F   U.S.-imposed economic sanctions against Iraq, Haiti, Bosnia, Serbia, and Cuba have had their desired effect.

33. T   F   The president decides whether to receive ambassadors.

34. T   F   Presidents have generally ignored the reporting requirements of the War Powers Resolution.

35. T   F   The popularity of foreign aid programs has increased in the United States since the mid-70s.

36. T   F   Madeleine Albright is the first woman secretary of state and the highest ranking woman in government.

37. T   F   The CIA's most important function is paramilitary maneuvers.

38. T   F   In general, a majority of Americans are well informed about foreign affairs.

39. T   F   Historically, American citizens have had little significant influence on the foreign policy created by their government.

Fill-in-the-Blanks

40. A pattern in which the United States fosters economic relations abroad without committing to strategic alliances that might draw the country into a war is called _____.

41. The view in which the U.S. sphere of influence has expanded beyond the Western Hemisphere to include virtually every corner of the globe where U.S. interests might be affected is called _____.

42. The disproportionate power that distinguished the United States and the Soviet Union from all other countries in the postwar era defines
_____.

43. U.S. foreign policy after 1946 was guided by the doctrine of _____, a concept delineated by George Kennan, then a State Department Soviet expert.

44. The bipolar struggle between the United States and the Soviet Union that began in the 1950s and ended in the 1990s was known as the
_____.

45. The _____ was a treaty signed by the Soviet Union and the eastern bloc in Europe agreeing to mutual defense, in reaction to NATO.

46. Richard Nixon initiated a policy of _____ in an attempt to relax the tensions between the United States and the Soviet Union through limited cooperation.

47. The _____ was signed by the United States (under President Nixon) and the Soviet Union to limit various classes of nuclear weapons.

48. The power that Congress has to oversee the operation of various federal agencies is called _____.

49. President Eisenhower in 1961 called the growing power and influence resulting from the conjunction of an immense military establishment and a large arms industry the _____.

Short Answer Essays

50. Explain the paradoxes of the concept of national interest.

51.   Describe the significant events occurring during the first era of U.S. foreign policy.

52.   Describe the significant events occurring during the second era of U.S. foreign policy.

53.   Describe the development of U.S. foreign policy from the end of the World War II to detente.

54.   Describe how and why U.S. foreign policy changed in 1989.

55.   Describe the important foreign policy issues since the breakup of the Soviet Union.

56.   List the Constitutional powers of the president and Congress in the area of foreign policy.

57.   Explain why the president has become preeminent in foreign affairs.

58.   Describe the constraints on Congress' ability to influence foreign policy.

59.   Give examples of Congress' impact on foreign policy through oversight.

60.   List the four core national-security areas and describe the organizations within each.

61.   Explain how the press and public opinion can act as a check on foreign-policy outcomes.

Answers

Chapter 1	Chapter 2	Chapter 3	Chapter 4
Multiple Choice	**Multiple Choice**	**Multiple Choice**	**Multiple Choice**
25. D	47. C	29. A	25. A
26. D	48. B	30. B	26. A
27. D	49. B	31. D	27. C
28. D	50. C	32. C	28. B
29. A	51. A	33. A	29. C
30. B	52. C	34. D	30. D
31. D	53. B	35. C	31. D
32. C	54. C	36. C	32. C
33. B	55. D	37. B	33. A
34. C	56. A	38. A	34. C
True/False	**True/False**	**True/False**	**True/False**
35. F	57. T	39. F	35. F
36. F	58. F	40. T	36. T
37. T	59. F	41. F	37. T
38. T	60. F	42. F	38. F
39. T	61. F	43. T	39. T
40. T	62. T	44. T	40. F
41. T	63. F	45. T	41. T
42. T	64. T	46. T	42. T
43. F	65. T	47. T	43. F
44. T	66. T	48. T	44. T
Fill-in-blanks	**Fill-in-blanks**	**Fill-in-blanks**	**Fill-in-blanks**
45. direct democracy	67. republic	49. states' rights	45.necessary and proper
46. republic	68. civil government	50. triad of powers	46. reapportionment
47. political discussion	69. limited government	51. carrot and stick	47. gerrymandering
48. negative freedom	70. Townshend Revenue Acts	52. supremacy	48. trustees
49. order, stability	71. Articles of Confederation	53. reserved powers	49. incumbents
50. shifting alliance	72. New Jersey Plan	54. police powers	50. term limits
51. universal suffrage	73. Electoral College System	55. nullification	51. Two Congresses
52. elections	74. Federalism	56. incorporation	52. subcommittees
53. right to privacy	75. Bill of Rights	57. federal mandate	53. pork barrel legislation
54. totalitarian	76. Democratic	58. grant-in-aid	54. congressional agenda

Chapter 5	Chapter 6	Chapter 7	Chapter 8
Multiple Choice	**Multiple Choice**	**Multiple Choice**	**Multiple Choice**
14. B	33. D	24. D	20. C
15. C	34. C	25. C	21. A
16. A	35. D	26. A	22. A
17. A	36. D	27. B	23. C
18. B	37. C	28. D	24. B
19. D	38. C	29. C	25. D
20. A	39. C	30. D	26. D
21. B	40. D	31. C	27. A
22. B	41. D	32. C	28. B
23. B	42. D	33. A	29. D
True/False	**True/False**	**True/False**	**True/False**
24. T	43. T	34. T	30. T
25. T	44. T	35. F	31. F
26. T	45. F	36. T	32. T
27. T	46. F	37. F	33. F
28. T	47. T	38. T	34. F
29. T	48. T	39. F	35. T
30. F	49. T	40. F	36. T
31. T	50. F	41. T	37. F
32. F	51. T	42. F	38. T
33. T	52. T	43. T	39. F
Fill-in-blanks	**Fill-in-blanks**	**Fill-in-blanks**	**Fill-in-blanks**
34. electoral college	53. appellate	44. hierarchy	40. representative sample
35. treaties	54. trial or petit	45. formal rules	41. question wording
36. executive agreements	55. class action	46. welfare state	42. tracking polls
37. rally effect	56. senatorial courtesy	47. spoils system	43. diversity, multi-culturalism
38. stewardship	57. docket	48. civil service	44. television
39. constructionists	58. rule of four	49. implementation	45. conservative
40. line item veto	59. opinion	50. cabinet department	46. liberty
41. War Powers Resolution	60. dissenting opinion	51. iron triangles	47. political ideology
42. chief of staff	61. stare decisis	52. senior executive service	48. schema
43. vice president	62. judicial activism	53. privatization	49. intensity

Chapter 9	Chapter 10	Chapter 11	Chapter 12
Multiple Choice	**Multiple Choice**	**Multiple Choice**	**Multiple Choice**
30. D	27. B	16. C	14. C
31. A	28. A	17. C	15. B
32. C	27. C	18. C	16. D
33. C	30. A	19. A	17. D
34. B	31. C	20. C	18. A
35. A	32. C	21. B	19. B
36. A	33. A	22. D	20. C
37. A	34. C	23. A	21. C
38. A	35. C	24. D	22. D
39. A	36. D	25. D	23. B
True/False	**True/False**	**True/False**	**True/False**
40. T	37. F	26. F	24. F
41. T	38. T	27. T	25. T
42. T	39. F	28. F	26. F
43. T	40. F	29. F	27. F
44. F	41. F	30. T	28. F
45. T	42. F	31. F	29. F
46. F	43. T	32. F	30. T
47. T	44. T	33. T	31. F
48. F	45. T	34. F	32. F
49. F	46. F	35. F	33. T
Fill-in-blanks	**Fill-in-blanks**	**Fill-in-blanks**	**Fill-in-blanks**
50. political parties	47. poll tax	36. diffusing	34. Independent Journal
51. Revolution of 1800	48. voter turnout	37. collective action	35. Time
52. King caucus	49. initiative	38. public interest groups	36. investigate journalism
53. primary system	50. straight-party	39. single issue	37. socialization
54. machine politics	51. retrospective voting	40. group maintenance	38. free press
55. party platform	52. mid-term elections	41. access	39. fairness doctrine
56. winner-take-all	53. faithless elector	42. direct mail	40. prior restraint
57. closed	54. maintaining	43. lobbying	41. symbiotic
58. superdelegate	55. soft money	44. soft money	42. horse race
59. electoral college	56. independent expenditures	45. David Truman	43. sound bites

Chapter 13	Chapter 14	Chapter 15	Chapter 16
Multiple Choice	**Multiple Choice**	**Multiple Choice**	**Multiple Choice**
22. C	27. A	17. D	27. A
23. B	28. C	18. C	28. A
24. B	29. D	19. D	29. C
25. C	30. B	20. B	30. C
26. C	31. D	21. B	31. A
27. C	32. A	22. C	32. C
28. C	33. C	23. A	33. D
29. C	34. D	24. D	34. C
30. D	35. C	25. A	35. D
31. B	36. D	26. C	36. B
True/False	**True/False**	**True/False**	**True/False**
32. T	37. F	27. T	37. F
33. F	38. F	28. F	38. T
34. T	39. T	29. F	39. T
35. F	40. T	30. F	40. F
36. F	41. T	31. T	41. F
37. T	42. T	32. T	42. T
38. T	43. T	33. T	43. T
39. T	44. T	34. F	44. F
40. T	45. T	35. F	45. F
41. T	46. F	36. T	46. T
Fill-in-blanks	**Fill-in-blanks**	**Fill-in-blanks**	**Fill-in-blanks**
42. incorporation	47. civil rights	37. regulatory policy	47. deficit
43. clear and present danger	48. de facto equality	38. life-cycle	48. fiscal policy
44. double jeopardy	49. de jure equality	39. policy agenda	49. Federal Reserve System
45. Lemon	50. Jim Crow	40. policy entrepreneur	50. stagflation
46. secular regulation	51. peonage	41. feedback loop	51. impoundment
47. fighting words	52. desegregation	42. environmental impact statement	52. Congressional Budget Office
48. hate speech	53. civil disobedience	43. Rio de Janiero, Brazil	53. tariffs
49. symbolic speech	54. boycotting	44. triggering mechanism	54. capital gains tax
50. prior restraint	55. affirmative action	45. Medicare Act	55. budget regulation
51. Miranda	56. equality of opportunity	46. Feminization of poverty	56. discretionary

Chapter 17

Multiple Choice
20. B
21. B
22. B
23. C
24. B
25. B
26. D
27. C
28. A
29. D

True/False
30. T
31. T
32. F
33. T
34. T
35. F
36. T
37. F
38. F
39. T

Fill-in-blanks
40. isolationism
41. globalism
42. superpower
43. containment
44. Cold War
45. Warsaw Pact
46. detente
47. Strategic Arms Limitation Treaty
48. legislative oversight
49. military-industrial complex